CONTENTS

JULES VERNE'S

AROUND THE WORLD IN
80 DAYS

A GRAPHIC NOVEL
BY CHRIS EVERHEART
& TOD SMITH

RAINTREE
A CAPSTONE COMPANY
PUBLISHERS FOR CHILDREN

Raintree is an imprint of Capstone Global Library
Limited, a company incorporated in England and
Wales having its registered office at 264 Banbury
Road, Oxford, OX2 7DY – Registered company
number: 6695582

www.raintree.co.uk
myorders@raintree.co.uk

British Library Cataloguing in Publication Data
A full catalogue record for this book is available from the
British Library.

Paperback ISBN: 978-1-4747-0390-1
Ebook ISBN: 978-1-4747-0395-6

Back matter written by Dr Katie Monnin

Maps credit: Dreamstime: Richard Thomas

Designer: Bob Lentz

Printed and bound in the United Kingdom.

ALL ABOUT AROUND THE WORLD IN 80 DAYS

Jules Verne's *Around the World in 80 Days* was first published in 1873. Originally written in French, the book's title was *Le tour du monde en quatre-vingts jours.* It has since been translated into nearly every language spoken on Earth and proven to be a classic all over the world.

During their approximately 80-day journey, Jean, Phileas and Aouda use a wide variety of transport, including trains, steamer ships, elephants and a wind-powered sledge (like a sailing boat that travels over snow).

Several obstacles get in their path, but like the industrial revolution at the time of Verne's writing, nothing can stop the near-locomotive force of Phileas Fogg's conviction and creativity in problem solving. With an iron will, they barrel through blockades and sneak past a determined detective with relative ease – and occasionally high risk.

Around the World in 80 Days is a story about travel, adventure and the industrial age. We follow the characters as they discover new lands, people and cultures. Perhaps that is why the book has been adapted for a wide variety of different media, including films, plays, musicals – and graphic novels like this one!

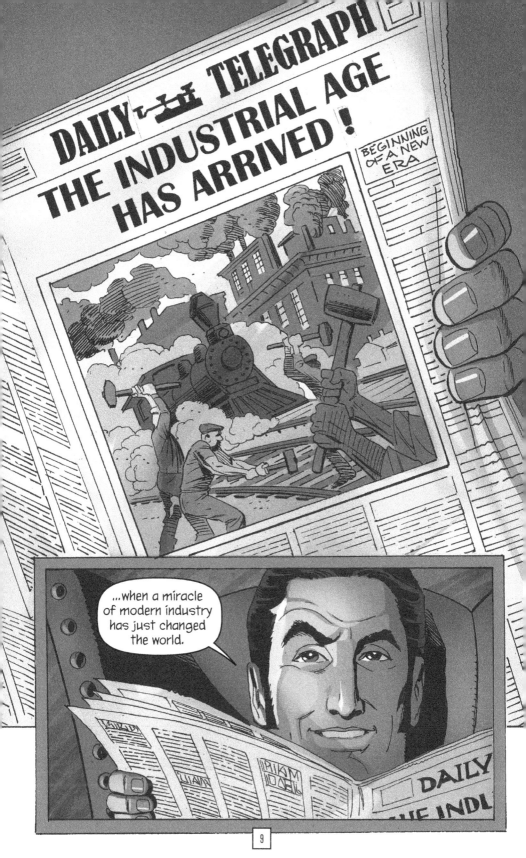

In seven days, Fogg and Jean managed to travel across Europe…

...and reach the Suez Canal, the new passage connecting ships to the Indian Ocean without navigating around Africa.

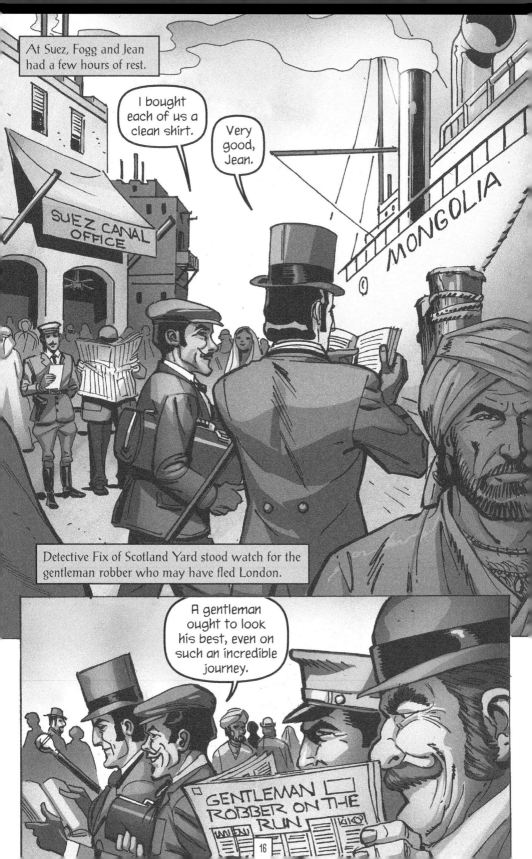

17

Deep in the belly of the Mongolia, men shovelled coal into the engine's furnace.

The water in the tank boiled, creating steam.

Steam ran through the pipes where the engineer set the flow.

LOW MEDIUM HIGH

Which cranked the piston…

…and drove the propeller that pushed the ship to Bombay.

CHAPTER 3
AOUDA

I BOUGHT an elephant. And I hired this man as our guide.

You've hired an elephant?!

No.

My name is Parsee.

And don't worry, sir, the elephant is mostly tame.

This will surely slow us down, Mr Fogg.

We're ahead of schedule, Jean. We gained two days on the ship from Suez to Bombay. We will be fine.

They camped overnight in the jungle.

At the station, Fix once again located his suspects.

Parsee, please keep this elephant as my gift. You've earned it.

You give me a great fortune, sir! Thank you!

Would you like to join us on our journey?

I have no family here. I would love to tour the world with you!

The *Rangoon* steamed towards Hong Kong, a 3,500 mile-long journey expected to take twelve days.

Jean made up for some missed meals.

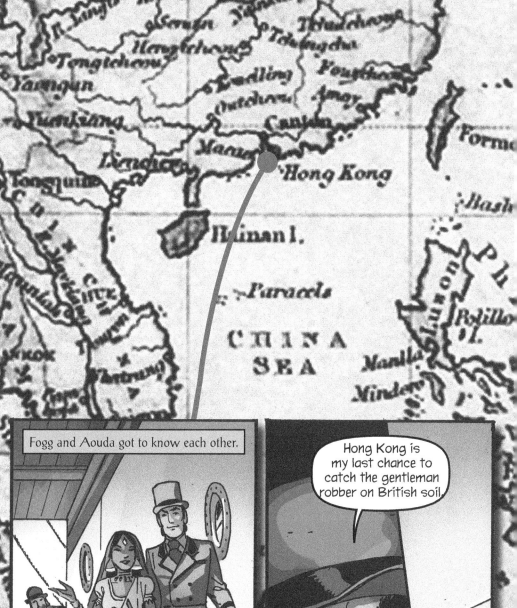

Fogg and Aouda got to know each other.

Hong Kong is my last chance to catch the gentleman robber on British soil.

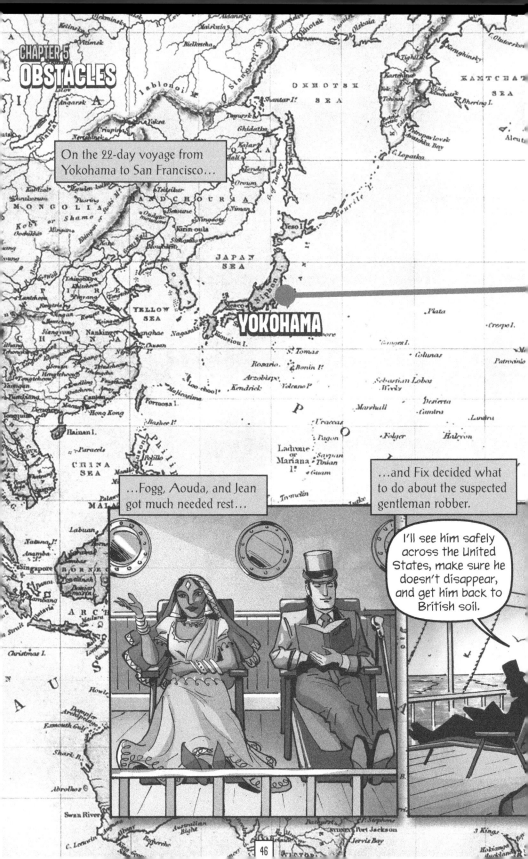

On the 22-day voyage from Yokohama to San Francisco…

YOKOHAMA

…and Fix decided what to do about the suspected gentleman robber.

…Fogg, Aouda, and Jean got much needed rest…

I'll see him safely across the United States, make sure he doesn't disappear, and get him back to British soil.

46

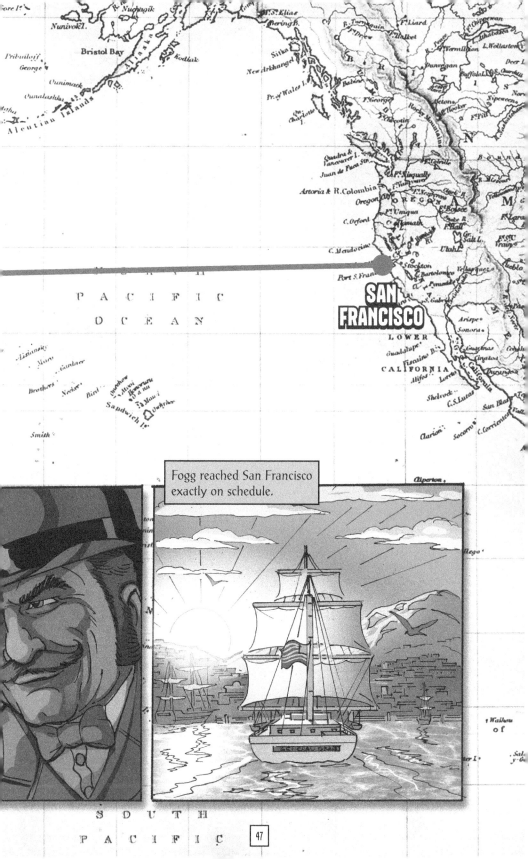

SAN FRANCISCO

Fogg reached San Francisco exactly on schedule.

After a day in San Francisco, they continued their journey on the Transcontinental railway.

Day and night the train chugged towards the heart of the United States.

49

SHWOOT SHWOOOOOT!

The locomotive powered forwards under full steam.

It reached the bridge at top speed…

CRASH!

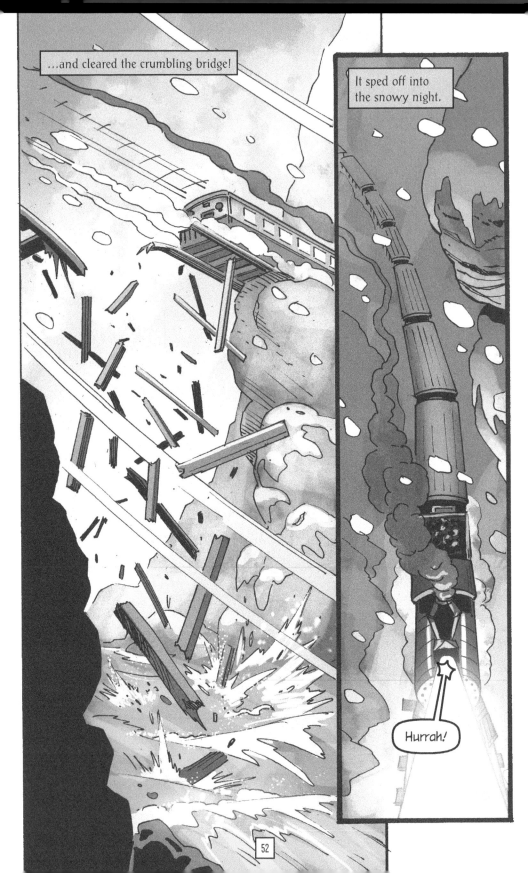

...only to be stopped again.

Only fifty miles to Omaha, but too much snow to continue.

FT. KEARNEY

Oh, why couldn't we have taken this part of the trip during summer?

The train isn't the only vehicle that crosses the Great Plains.

FT. KEA

They reached New York on the 11th, as planned.

NEW YORK CITY

Mr Fogg, we're here!

And right on time, Jean.

Yes, Mr Fogg, and your last chance to disappear in the United States.

Fogg found an energy source underfoot.

Captain, sell me your ship.

TAP! TAP!

CRUNCH! SNAP!

SAW!

Straight to the furnace. Every piece of wood is fuel now.

With the coal gone, the wood kept the boiler at full steam.

On 21 December, a vessel that was once a ship docked at Liverpool harbour.

More than enough time – and just enough money left to buy our train tickets.

It's six hours by train to London, sir!

I've worked out your game at last. And I don't need a warrant because I have proof!

I don't know what you mean, Mr Fix.

Just a moment!

ABOUT THE AUTHOR AND ILLUSTRATOR OF THIS RETELLING

Chris Everheart always dreamt of interesting places, fascinating people and exciting adventures. He is still a dreamer. He enjoys writing thrilling stories about young heroes who live in a world that doesn't always understand them. Chris lives in Minnesota, USA, with his family. He plans to travel to every continent on the globe, see interesting places, meet fascinating people and have exciting adventures – much like Phileas Fogg and his companions!

Tod Smith is a self-employed illustrator and a graduate of the Joe Kubert School of Cartooning and Graphic Art. He has illustrated a wide variety of books, including work for companies, such as Marvel. He currently lives in Connecticut, USA.

GLOSSARY

arrest to use the power of the law to take and keep someone in custody

boiler a large container in which water is heated to produce steam in an engine

piston a part of an engine that moves up and down inside a tube, causing other parts of the engine to move

propeller a device with two or more blades that turn quickly and cause a ship or aircraft to move

rajah a king or prince in India

ritual a formal ceremony or series of acts that is always performed in the same way

sacrifice an act of killing a person or animal in a religious ceremony to please a god

tame not wild, or trained to obey people

warrant a document issued by a court that gives the police the power to do something, like arrest someone

READING QUESTIONS

1. Why do the characters go on an eighty-day journey around the world?

2. List all the different methods of transportation that Jean and Phileas take on their journey. Next, write down a few advantages and disadvantages of each particular form of travel.

3. Make a list of all the obstacles the characters in this book face on their journey. How do they overcome their obstacles?

WRITING PROMPTS

1. Draw a map that includes a destination the group travels to in this book. Then write a description of the location. What did the characters experience there?

2. Imagine you are one of the characters in this book. Write a postcard to a friend or a family member about your journey. What will you tell them about?

3. Write four paragraphs about your favourite character. Why do you like that character the most? Identify areas in the text and illustrations that show why you like the character.

READ THEM ALL!

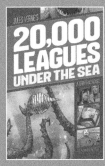

JULES VERNE'S
20,000 LEAGUES
UNDER THE SEA

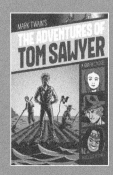

MARK TWAIN'S
THE ADVENTURES OF
TOM SAWYER

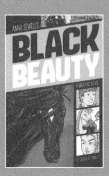

ANNA SEWELL'S
BLACK BEAUTY

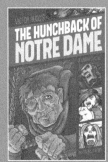

VICTOR HUGO'S
THE HUNCHBACK OF
NOTRE DAME

ROBIN HOOD

ROBERT LOUIS STEVENSON'S
TREASURE ISLAND

MARY SHELLEY'S
FRANKENSTEIN

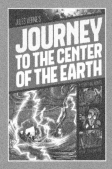

JULES VERNE'S
JOURNEY
TO THE CENTER
OF THE EARTH

H. G. WELLS'S
THE WAR OF THE WORLDS

ROBERT LOUIS STEVENSON'S
THE STRANGE CASE OF
DR. JEKYLL
AND MR. HYDE

WASHINGTON IRVING'S
THE LEGEND OF SLEEPY HOLLOW

BRAM STOKER'S
DRACULA

DANIEL DEFOE'S
ROBINSON CRUSOE

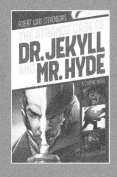

CHARLES DICKENS'S
A CHRISTMAS CAROL

JONATHAN SWIFT'S
GULLIVER'S TRAVELS

ARTHUR CONAN DOYLE'S
THE HOUND OF THE BASKERVILLES

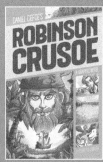

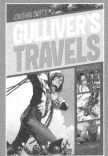

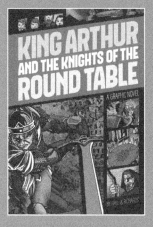

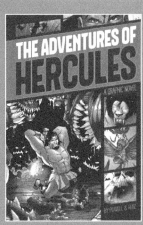